P9-COO-882

A Home in the Swamp

By David C. Lion

Children's Press®
A Division of Scholastic Inc.
New York Toronto London Auckland Sydney
Mexico City New Delhi Hong Kong
Danbury, Connecticut

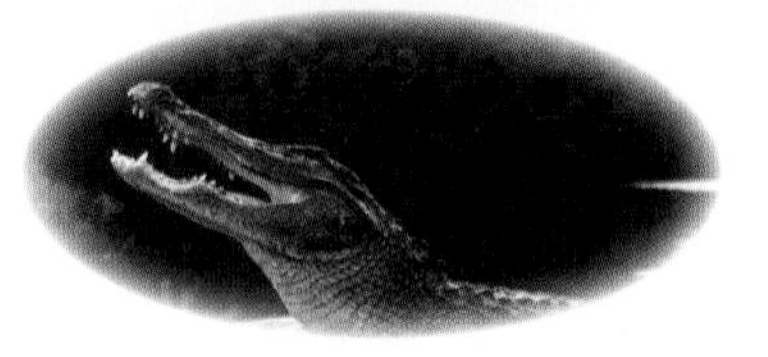

These content vocabulary word builders are for grades 1–2.
Subject Consultant: Susan Woodward, Professor of Geography, Radford University, Radford, Virginia

Reading Consultant: Cecilia Minden-Cupp, PhD, Former Director of the Language and Literacy Program, Harvard Graduate School of Education, Cambridge, Massachusetts

Photographs © 2007: Animals Animals: 15 (C.C. Lockwood), cover background (Brian K. Miller), 21 top (Robert Winslow), 20 bottom (Maria Zorn); Corbis Images/Markus Botzek/zefa: 23 bottom right; Dembinsky Photo Assoc.: 5 top right, 8 (Bill Lea), 23 top left (Doug Locke), cover left inset, 5 top left, 6 (Gary Meszaros), cover center inset, 5 bottom right, 11 (Ted Nelson); Minden Pictures/Gerry Ellis: 19; NHPA/James Carmichael Jr.: back cover, 5 bottom left, 9; Peter Arnold Inc./A. & J. Visage: 2, 13; Photo Researchers, NY: cover right inset, 4 bottom left, 17 (Joseph T. and Suzanne L. Collins), 1, 4 bottom right, 7 (Gregory G. Dimijian), 23 bottom left, 23 top right (Thomas & Pat Leeson); The Image Works/Eastcott/Momatiuk: 4 top, 16; Tom Stack & Associates, Inc./Therisa Stack: 21 bottom; TRIP Photo Library/Helene Rogers: 20 top.

Book Design: Simonsays Design!
Book Production: The Design Lab

Library of Congress Cataloging-in-Publication Data

Lion, David C., 1948-
A home in the swamp / by David C. Lion.
p. cm. — (Scholastic news nonfiction readers)
Includes index.
ISBN-10: 0-516-25349-2
ISBN-13: 978-0-516-25349-7
1. Swamp ecology—Juvenile literature. I. Title. II. Series.
QH541.5.S9L56 2006
577.68—dc22 2006002885

1 2 3 4 5 6 7 8 9 10 R 16 15 14 13 12 11 10 09 08 07

CONTENTS

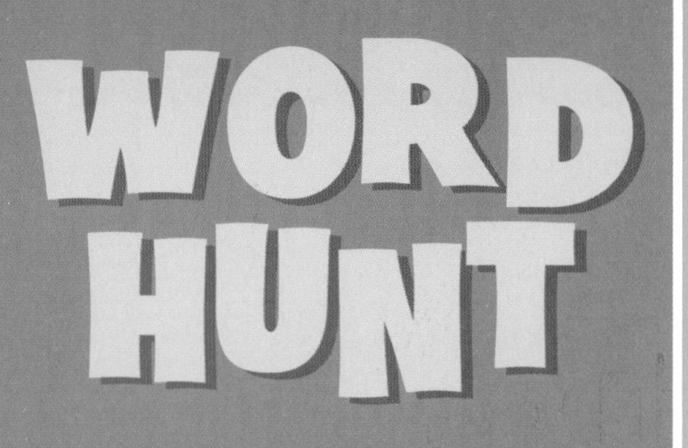

Look for these words as you read. They will be in **bold**.

crayfish
(**kray**-fish)

pig frogs
(**pig frogs**)

Spanish moss
(**spa**-nish **mohss**)

dragonfly
(**drah**-guhn-fly)

habitat
(**hab**-uh-tat)

swamp
(**swahmp**)

wood ducks
(**wud ducks**)

What Is This Place?

The air and ground are warm and damp. **Spanish moss** hangs above your head.

A **dragonfly** zooms past. Where are we?

Spanish moss hangs from trees that grow in the water.

We're in a **swamp** in the southern United States!

A swamp is a type of **habitat**. A habitat is where a plant or animal usually lives.

The air there is warm. The ground is wet and spongy.

habitat

Many trees in swamps grow in the water.

Wood ducks live in the swamp. These ducks eat small fish, insects, water plants, acorns, and berries.

Snapping turtles live there, too. They eat baby wood ducks. They also hunt fish, frogs, and snakes.

Wood ducks build nests in holes in the trees.

Alligators are the largest animals in the swamp.

So where does a 400-pound alligator build its home? Anywhere it wants!

Alligators have eighty teeth!

An alligator builds its home by digging a hole with its snout and tail. These holes are called gator holes. Gator holes fill with water.

An alligator's coloring helps it blend in with its surroundings.

Pig frogs live in the swamp, too. These frogs eat mostly **crayfish** and insects.

Pig frogs get their name from the loud grunting sounds they make.

The swamp is an exciting place to explore! Hop in a canoe, and watch out for those alligators. You'll meet these flamingos and other amazing animals that live in this habitat!

A DAY IN THE LIFE OF AN ALLIGATOR

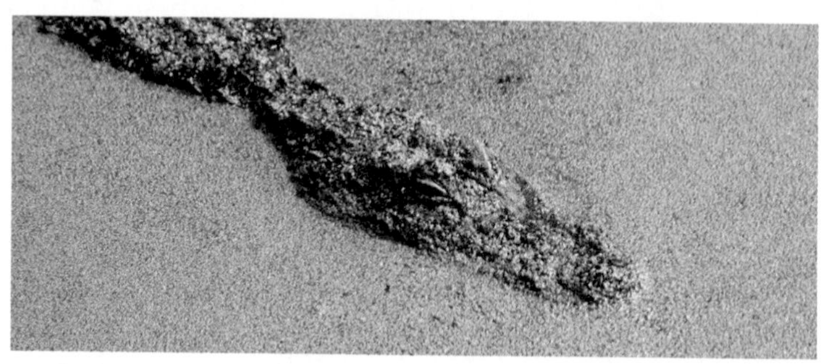

How does an alligator spend most of its time? An alligator soaks in ponds, lakes, or gator holes.

What does an alligator eat? An alligator eats fish, frogs, snakes, birds, raccoons, opossums, and sometimes even other alligators.

What are an alligator's enemies? Other alligators and humans are an alligator's enemies.

Does an alligator have a special survival trick? An alligator blends in with its surroundings. An alligator is brownish-green. When it stays very still, it almost looks like a log!

YOUR NEW WORDS

crayfish (**kray**-fish) animals that look like lobsters but are usually much smaller

dragonfly (**drah**-guhn-fly) a flying insect with a long, skinny body that usually lives near water

habitat (**hab**-uh-tat) the place where a plant or animal usually lives

pig frogs (**pig frogs**) large, active frogs that hunt at night

Spanish moss (**spa**-nish **mohss**) a flowering plant that hangs from tree branches

swamp (**swahmp**) a wetland with damp, spongy ground

wood ducks (**wud ducks**) ducks that make their nests in trees

OTHER ANIMALS THAT LIVE IN THE SWAMP

beavers

otters

panthers

sandhill crane

FIND OUT MORE

Book:

Gibbons, Gail. *Marshes and Swamps.* New York: Holiday House, 1998.

Website:

Science News for Kids: Saving Wetlands
http://www.sciencenewsforkids.org/articles/20050406/Feature1.asp

MEET THE AUTHOR:

David Lion is a retired school teacher and author of children's books. He lives with his wife, Kathy, and their cat, Jeep, in Glens Falls, New York. When not writing, David can be found on his bass boat, on the golf course, or reading to his granddaughter.